Abraham Lincoln
에이브러햄 링컨

Biography Comic
who? ⑨ Abraham Lincoln

개정판 1쇄 인쇄 2014년 3월 5일
개정판 1쇄 발행 2014년 3월 10일

글 안형모
그림 스튜디오 청비
번역 하이엔 박
감수 김수희
펴낸이 김선식

책임편집 김선영 **디자인** 박효영
콘텐츠개발팀장 김선영 **콘텐츠개발팀** 박효영, 이유미, 김선민, 조서인
마케팅본부 이상혁

펴낸곳 스튜디오 다산 **출판등록** 2013년 11월 1일 제414-81-37694
주소 경기도 파주시 회동길 37-14 3층
전화 02-702-1724(기획편집) 02-703-1725(마케팅) 02-704-1724(경영관리)
팩스 02-703-2219 **who클럽** cafe.naver.com/dasankids
종이 월드페이퍼(주) | **인쇄** (주)현문 | **제본** 광성문화사

ISBN 979-11-5639-031-2 (14740)

who?
Abraham
Lincoln
에이브러햄 링컨

글 **이수정** | 그림 **스튜디오 청비** | 번역 **하이엔 박** | 감수 **김수희**

Dasan Kid

Abraham Lincoln

**The 16th President of the United States of America,
February 12 1809~April 15 1865**

Abraham Lincoln, one of the most respected Presidents by the American people for his role as a protector of freedom and peace, was born on February 12, 1809 in a small log cabin in Kentucky. He was born the son of a poor settler and received almost no formal education. However, by reading books, he was able to achieve his dreams.

During his adolescence, Lincoln, by chance, witnessed an event at a slave market where slaves were sold and bought like property. He was extremely shocked by what he saw. As always, following his own convictions, Lincoln spoke out and openly criticized the institution of slavery. Through such speeches, Lincoln became instantly famous. Thus, in 1861, Lincoln was elected as the 16th President of the United States of America.

However, as soon as Lincoln made his way to assume the Presidency, the pro-slavery states left the Union in succession to form the Confederate States of America. Thereafter, to preserve the Union and unite the country, the Civil War was started.

Lincoln issued the Emancipation Proclamation on January 1, 1863. With this, not only the black slaves but also all slaves in the states that had left the Union became free. Lincoln gained much support from the people and was reelected in the 1864 Presidential Election amidst the Civil War.

Finally, in April 1865, the Civil War came to an end with the surrender by the South's commander-in-chief, General Robert E. Lee. However, a few days later, in the evening of April 14, 1865, Lincoln was shot by John Wilkes Booth in the Ford's Theater in Washington, D.C. and passed away the next morning.

Abraham Lincoln, as a man, may have disappeared into history, but as a symbol of freedom and equality, he lives on in the hearts of many through his works and through his visionary words - "Government of the people, by the people, for the people, shall not perish from the Earth."

에이브러햄 링컨

미국 16대 대통령, 1809년 2월 12일~1865년 4월 15일

자유와 평화의 수호자로서 미국인들에게 가장 존경받는 대통령인 에이브러햄 링컨은 1809년 2월 12일, 켄터키 주의 작은 통나무집에서 태어났습니 다 . 그는 가난한 개척자의 아들로 정규 교육은 거의 받지 못했지만 독서를 통해 꿈을 키웠습니다.

링컨은 청년 시절 우연히 흑인 노예들을 사고파는 노예 시장을 보고 큰 충격을 받습니다. 링컨은 평소 자신의 소신대로 이에 반대하며 노예제를 정면으로 비판하는 연설을 합니다. 이 일로 링컨은 순식간에 유명 인물로 부각되었고 1861년 미국 제 16대 대통령으로 당선됩니다.

그러나 노예제를 반대하는 링컨이 대통령에 오르자 노예제를 찬성하는 주들이 잇달아 미합중국을 이탈하여 연합국을 세웁니다. 이로 인해 미국을 통일하기 위한 남북 전쟁이 시작되었습니다.

링컨은 1863년 1월 1일, 노예 해방 선언문을 발표합니다. 그에 따라 흑인뿐만 아니라 미국 전역의 노예들이 자유의 몸이 됩니다. 사람들의 지지를 얻은 링컨은 전쟁 중인 1864년 대통령 선거에서 재선에 성공합니다.

결국 1865년 4월, 남군 총사령관 리 장군이 항복함으로써 남북 전쟁은 종결되었습니다. 그러나 링컨은 며칠 후인 1865년 4월 14일 저녁, 워싱턴의 포드 극장에서 존 윌크스 부스의 총에 맞아 다음날 아침 세상을 떠납니다.

에이브러햄 링컨은 역사 속으로 사라졌지만 자유와 평등을 상징하는 "국민의, 국민에 의한, 국민을 위한 정부는 지구상에서 영원히 사라지지 않을 것입니다."라는 연설은 많은 이들의 가슴속에 기억되고 있습니다.

이 책을 만든 사람들

글 · 이수정

우연히 접한 학습 만화의 매력에 푹 빠져서 어려운 내용을 어린이들의 눈높이에 맞게 쉽고 재미있게 설명할 수 있는 학습 만화 시나리오를 쓰게 되었습니다. 겉으로 보이는 위인들의 훌륭한 면뿐만 아니라 숨겨진 노력과 열정을 찾아내어 감동적인 이야기를 만들기 위해 노력합니다.

그림 · 스튜디오 청비

기발한 상상력을 바탕으로 새롭고 재미있는 콘텐츠를 만들어 내는 만화 창작 집단입니다. 어린이들이 책을 읽고 큰 꿈을 품기를 바라는 마음으로 즐겁게 작업하고 있습니다. 작품으로 『성철 스님』, 『아 다르고 어 다른 우리말 101가지』, 『반기문 유엔 사무총장의 꿈과 도전』 등이 있습니다.

번역 · 하이엔 박(Hyanne Sue Park)

미국 시카고에서 태어났으며, 스텐퍼드 대학에서 사회학 전공으로 학사, 석사 학위를 받았습니다. USC Law School 졸업 후, 가정폭력 담당 변호사로 일했습니다. 현재 한국에서 영어를 가르치며 비영리 단체를 위해 영어 통역사로 일하고 있습니다.

감수 · 김수희

연세대학교에서 역사를 전공했습니다. 이후 한국뿐 아니라 일본, 미국에서 한국어, 일본어, 영어를 가르쳐 왔으며 부모를 위한 영어교육용 책을 썼습니다. 영어교육채널 EBSe '엄마표 영어특강'에서 강의를 하며 홈스쿨, 알파벳과 파닉스, 다차원 테마 영어 수업 기법을 알리고 있습니다. 전국 각지에서 어린이 영어 교육에 대한 강연을 하며 창의적이고 열정적인 교수법으로 영어를 배우고자 하는 어린이와 부모들에게 많은 도움을 주고 있습니다.

Abraham Lincoln

Which speech is Lincoln famous for, which poignantly calls for democracy and is known for the phrase, "government of the people, by the people, for the people?"

a. Gettysburg Address
b. Pittsburg Address
c. Southern Address

Answer:a

Contents

01   A Gift from Mother   10

02   Abe, the Bookworm   30

03   An Honest Fellow   48

04   Jumping into Politics   72

 From a Log Cabin to the White House 92

 The Civil War 110

 The Emancipation Proclamation 132

 The Legacy of Freedom and Equality 152

Workbook 168

01 • A Gift from Mother

 Track 01 ▶

In a tiny log cabin in the State of Kentucky, Abraham Lincoln was born on February 12, 1809 as a son of a poor settler. The family called him Abe.

Mother, please tell me a Bible story.

Every night before going to bed, his deeply devoted mother told him Bible stories. This was Abraham's favorite part of the whole day.

Okay, I'll tell you a story from Deuteronomy.

Be strong and courageous. Do not be afraid or terrified because of them.

Abraham's father, Thomas Lincoln, did not know how to read or write, but he was a very hardworking and honest person.

His mother, Nancy Lincoln, who also could not read, was a very kind and wise woman.

You'd better go to sleep now since we have to go to the fields early tomorrow.

"For the Lord your God goes with you."

Young Abe owned neither a picture book nor a decent toy to play with, but he never said a word of complaint and was a good-natured, kindhearted boy.

The Lincoln family searched for better farmland and worked without rest from morning to late at night, but they could not overcome their poverty. Abraham and his older sister, Sarah, helped their parents around the farm by either planting seeds or carrying rocks.

Eventually, after much persuasion on their mother's part, their father, who at first had opposed, agreed to send them to school.

Although the whole school consisted of only one teacher and one classroom, Abraham loved going to school.

Father, Mother, I'm home from school!

Lad, slow down. You might fall!

Heh-heh!

You like school that much?

Yes, Mother! Studying is fun, too!

14

When there was a lot of farm work to be done, they missed more days at school because the family was short-handed. Abraham felt sad about this, but he never felt resentment toward his parents.

Track 04 ▶

Harvest is almost over, so now we should slowly start preparing to leave.

We're leaving?

Abe, he means "We're moving."

But, I like it here...

This land is too parched and barren. No crop could grow well here. We need to find fertile land.

I'm worried. Soon it'll be winter.

The Lincoln family left in search of a more fertile land. After an exhausting one-month journey, the Lincolns finally arrived in the state of Indiana, located in the Midwest.

Let's leave before then.

By the summer, a mysterious illness swept through the community. It was called "milk sickness", and was contracted by drinking milk from cows that grazed on poisonous plants. It was a devastating disease that had no cure.

I understand, but you be careful too.

I will.

Darling, I'm going to visit my relatives to take care of them. They are sick.

Sis, could you read me the Bible, please?

But I still do not know how to read well.

Please be quiet and go to sleep, both of you!

Phew, I wish I could go back to school.

20

After a few days, Mother returned with a dark expression on her face.

What shall I do? How could they pass away first, leaving behind a young child…

How many times should we endure such things?

Mother, are you okay?

Ye…Yes. I'm all right.

23

I hope you will become a person whose life follows the truth of the Bible. Please... do not strive to become a wealthy landowner.

Don't go, Mother! You can't die.

My beloved son, please become an upright and honest person.

Thomas, please take good care of our children.

No, Nancy!

When Abraham was
nine years old, his mother died
of the milk sickness.
The family was overwhelmed
with unbearable grief.

Mother!

Don't leave me,
Mother!

There was no sound of laughter or happiness in a house where their mother no longer existed. Heartbroken Abraham no longer said much or played with other children.

Sarah had to take over all the household chores and caring for the family, but it was just too much for an eleven-year-old girl. The house slowly became messy and dirty.

Abe, where are you going?

Whenever Abraham missed his mother, he visited her gravesite.

I miss you so much, Mother. What will I do without you?

Abe, don't cry.

28

02 Abe, the Bookworm

(CD1) Track 11 ▶

A little over a year after his mother's death, Abraham's father remarried and brought home a stepmother.

Here is your new mother who will live with us from now on.

Sarah Bush Johnston, their stepmother, was a cheerful and sweet person. She showed a lot of compassion and kindness to the Lincoln siblings, and Abraham quickly grew to love his stepmother.

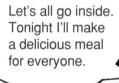

Let's all go inside. Tonight I'll make a delicious meal for everyone.

Their hardworking stepmother brought cleanliness and order into the home. Life and excitement returned to the house. Abraham and Sarah regained their strength and cheerful dispositions.

It's a book!

♫

Abe, I'm so glad to know you love books.

I do...If only I could read, heh-heh.

Heavens! You still haven't learned to read? You must attend school right away.

Father wouldn't like it.

Don't worry about that. You must study diligently!

Yes, Mother!

Abe, Father has consented. From tomorrow, you can go to school.

Really? Thank you, thank you!

Abraham started to attend a school that was about two miles away from home. To young Lincoln, this was a far distance to walk, but at the thought of learning how to read, he did not consider it one bit strenuous.

Abraham was very bright. If he learned something once, he never forgot it. Because he also had tremendous tenacity and an insatiable curiosity to learn, he wanted to know everything. He would only be satisfied if he found the answers to things that puzzled him.

Why aren't you eating? What are you looking at so intensely?

Leave him alone. Now that he has learned how to read, he has so many books he wants to read.

What a waste of time and energy!

But that's not true. Father, we can gain so much knowledge by reading books.

Be quiet! And, don't even think about going to school tomorrow. Instead you'll help me in the fields.

Okay, I understand.

Abraham always had a book in his hands. He would read and study every chance he got between chores. When he read books, he made sure to write down in his notebook all the stories and Bible passages that impressed him. In fact he developed a habit of writing down even the smallest things.

Phew, let's return home now.

Abe, now that our family has grown in numbers, it's getting too hard to provide for them just through farm work. I'm sorry to request this of you, but can you quit school and help out the family?

Yes, I can do that. I have already learned how to read and do arithmetic. I guess that's enough...

I'm so sorry to ask this of you.

Oh no, Father. I should have helped out much sooner…

Abraham wanted to pursue his studies further, but he did not show his disappointment. He was a good son who put his father's wishes and concerns before his.

School is not the only place I can learn…

Because of helping out so much on the farm, Abraham was absent from school more days than he attended. His entire schooling amounted to less than one year. That short period was Abraham's total formal education he received before becoming the President.

36

Abraham began to study on his own. Books became his teachers. Whether he was working hard or resting under the shade of a tree between chores, he always had a book with him to read.

Abraham had many books he wanted to read, but had no money to buy them. Thus, he mostly borrowed books from neighbors.

Soon after he had read all the books in his town, he even walked for miles to distant neighborhoods to borrow more books.

39

This is really interesting. Wow!

What am I going to do? The book's soaked from the rain.

Phew, I must tell Mr. Crawford the truth and beg for forgiveness.

The first book
I've ever owned!
Hurray!

03 An Honest Fellow

CD1 Track 20 ▶

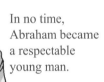

In no time, Abraham became a respectable young man.

Later, Sarah, Elizabeth, and Matilda all left home after getting married. At home, it was just Abraham, his younger brother, John, and his parents. To help support his large family who was still financially struggling, he took on whatever job that earned him money.

He picked fruit in the orchards, he built log cabins for new settlers, and he even took on all kinds of odds-and-ends jobs in his town.

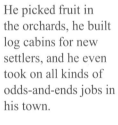

Do you know this story?

There once was a criminal who was about to be executed. So one winter day, the prison guard told this criminal that he would grant him one wish.

Despite hardships, Abraham always remained good-natured. With his amazing storytelling gift and confidence, he never failed to entertain everyone around him, including his fellow workers. In fact, his honesty was the talk of the town. Everyone in town knew he had a good reputation.

Abraham, long time no see.

How have you been?

Me? It's always the same. I'm glad that I ran into you. Do you know how to row?

Yes, sir.

Have you ever thought about being a ferryman?

I would love to be one, but what about you? You're the best ferryman in town!

I'm moving soon, and I want someone like you who is hardworking and honest to take over my business.

If that's the case, I'll be happy to do it.

Thank you, Abraham.

Abraham felt very comfortable in his new job as a ferryman, helping passengers to cross the river.

You have a lot of cargo. I'll load them up. Heave-ho!

How kind of you.

So kind... And he has a strong sense of responsibility. Such a rare lad.

Not only that, he can readily handle any work given to him and he is so hardworking!

I need to deliver some cargo to New Orleans. I'll compensate you well. What do you think?

New Orleans? It would take a good 3 months.

Look, the travel may be dangerous, but for that reason, I need someone I can trust.

I would love to.

But it'll be difficult by yourself.

I'll talk to my brother and my cousin. Maybe they can help me.

Abraham, his stepbrother, John Johnston, and his cousin, John Hanks, loaded up the cargo on the flatboat and headed for New Orleans.

What is New Orleans like?

Compared to here, it's completely different. Probably, you'll see a whole new world.

A whole new world? Suddenly, I feel my heart racing!

Abraham's traveling crew was utterly exhausted from their long, weary voyage.

John, hurry up and row.

Okay!

And you, bail water out of the boat.

I'll do my best.

Mr. Offutt, we have to throw some cargo overboard. As a temporary measure, we must reduce the weight to buy us some time until I can find a place to land this boat.

Let's do that.

It's going to be tough to repair this.

The boat must have struck something…

Don't worry. I'll try to fix it.

Mr. Offutt, it's fixed!

Thank you! You're something else!

After some difficulties, Abraham's crew finally arrived in New Orleans.

Everyone, thank you for all your hard work.

Abraham, thanks to you, we arrived safely.

No problem at all, sir!

Abraham, after you return home, make sure you stop by my store.

Abe, do we have to leave so soon? Let's look around a bit.

I agree. We came all this way. Let's do a little sightseeing.

Seeing this splendid city for the first time was very exciting for Abraham.

Wouldn't it be great to live here?

Amazing!

A place like this would have a lot of job opportunities.

Huh? What's going on there?

There, for the first time, Abraham witnessed a shocking, horrible event.

Must be a circus? Let's go see.

For sale - a very vigorous, hardworking slave. Name your price!

This can't be!

Abraham's heart felt so overwhelmed with compassion and pity for the slaves he saw. It became unbearable for him to think of their plight.
Even after he returned home, their cries rang in his ears.
The image of the little slave girl who died so tragically generated many emotions in Abraham.

This isn't right! This horrible, cruel institution of slavery must be abolished. Unjust laws must be changed!

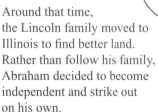

In 1831, Abraham turned 21 years old and began working at Mr. Denton Offutt's store in New Salem, Illinois.
Customers began to like and trust Abraham who dealt with them honestly and with a humble attitude.

Around that time, the Lincoln family moved to Illinois to find better land. Rather than follow his family, Abraham decided to become independent and strike out on his own.

That's right! It's time for me to set out and see this world for myself!

I have to return it right away. Sir, I'll be back.

This late at night? Look, it won't be too late to go in the morning to return it and apologize.

Although it was just a few cents, Abraham believed that the right thing to do was to return the money to the customer. Through the pitch black night, he walked for more than 6 miles.

I'm sorry it's late but…

What is the store clerk doing here so late?

Didn't you purchase a bag of flour this afternoon from our store?

Ye…Yes.

I'll make sure this doesn't happen again. Please accept our sincerest apologies!

I gave you the wrong change by mistake. I'm so sorry!

Good heavens! You came all this way at such a late hour to return this to me?

04 Jumping into Politics

🎧CD1 Track 32 ▶

The townspeople persuaded Lincoln to run for a seat in the state legislature. He was hesitant at first, but gradually became interested in the idea.

Do I have the qualifications to run for office? Maybe... And I want to do something meaningful for all the people in my state!

With firm determination, Lincoln ran for the state legislature in 1832.

Abraham Lincoln

I'm currently a store clerk.

I have no wealth, and I haven't had much schooling. However, I shall be a faithful servant who will be unrelenting in my duties for our district.

During Lincoln's election campaign, there was a movement by the Indians to occupy the state of Illinois. To end the uprising, the Governor of Illinois called upon the militia. Lincoln enlisted and fought for his state. Thus, he had no time to campaign for the election.

What a shame, he ran off without paying his debts.

After returning home from his military duties, he had no job waiting for him. He had lost the state legislature election, and Denton Offutt had closed his store.

Hello, how have you been?

Who knew Mr. Offutt would do such a thing?

Hey, Abraham! Long time no see.

It's a pity about the last election. And even Mr. Offutt has run off… Must be disappointing that you weren't elected!

Whatever you say! Anyway, don't work too hard.

Heh-heh. Finally, I can drink without you nagging me!

His alcoholism has relapsed! I'm worried!

Before long, Lincoln was appointed as postmaster. Because he was the sole employee, he not only had to serve the customers, receiving letters and packages at the post office, but also had to deliver all the mail in person.

Ultimately, the store failed and they were left with a $1,000 debt. On top of that, Lincoln's partner, Berry, died in an accident leaving the entire debt to Lincoln.

Are you trying to take off with my money?

I trusted you, but I see that I've misjudged you.

I'm sorry.

You think saying sorry is enough? Give me back my money now!

If you give me some time, I'll work to pay off the debt. No matter what, I promise you that I'll pay it all back.

How can we trust your words? Are you trying to buy time to run off like the others?

Hmph, when on earth would you pay off that debt?

Now, no one even trusts me.

We might as well take whatever is left!

You'd better not think of running away!

At the time, there were many people who were fleeing as soon as their business failed. Once a person left the district where the debt was acquired, he did not have to repay it. People thought Lincoln would also run off because $1,000 during that time was such a huge sum of money. It would have been difficult to earn that amount in most people's lifetime.

Lincoln did not flee like a coward. Instead, he remained in New Salem and took on whatever work he could find to repay the debt. Seeing how hard Lincoln was working to repay his debts, even the creditors, who were once impatiently hounding him for the money, eased off. Through this incident, Lincoln's integrity was affirmed once again in people's eyes.

If I work hard, I'll pay off the debt sooner or later.

Everyone appreciates a hard day's work. I'll get started right away!

Track 38 ▶

Then, in 1834, Lincoln ran for office once again, but this time in a more favorable position than he did two years ago.

However, he did not have money for his campaign. So, he personally canvassed for votes on foot, running from voters to voters. Wherever there were people, he was there to meet them and share his ideas with them.

I have a dream of building a commonwealth where its poor and powerless can have a better life.

How could a young person like yourself build such a commonwealth?

We're busy working, so, stop talking nonsense and get out of here!

I understand your hearts and concerns better than anyone.

Before I learned how to walk, I learned to farm first!

HA HA HA

If the qualification of the state representative you want is of this sort, am I not qualified?

What excellent hand skills!

If we were rude, we are sorry. Our words were too harsh. I promise to vote for you.

Thank you so much!

Hey, hey! Leaving so soon?

Huh?

If you're not too busy, lend us a hand?

I was just about to ask if I could help! Ha-ha-ha!

HA HA HA

Those who really got to know Lincoln's true nature threw their support behind him. In November 1834, Lincoln was elected to the state legislature.

Thank you very much, everyone! I'll work hard and do my best!

Congratulations, Representative!

Cheers for Representative Lincoln!

After becoming a state representative, Lincoln decided to become a lawyer to be a better politician. He began studying law with the help of a fellow legislator, John T. Stuart.

Isn't this an unfair measure?

If you decide to get into politics, you must acquire in-depth knowledge of the law.

I need to study law.

I agree. Take this opportunity to study hard and take the bar exam. I'll help you.

Thank you. I'll study hard!

Ma'am, please take this money back.

Oh, no! Please accept it as your consultation fee.

I can't take this from you since I only did what I'm supposed to do.

Really?

Lincoln became well-known as an honest and sincere lawyer. In Springfield, there was not a person who didn't know his name.

Mr. Lincoln, thank you. Thank you very much!

Oh, no, please don't thank me! It's obvious that you were freed because you were not guilty.

Thank you.

Good work!

Thanks. Well, I'll turn in for the night.

Where do you think you're going? Did you forget that we have somewhere to go tonight?

NO- NO- NO!

At a social event for Springfield's young socialites, Lincoln and Mary Todd fell in love at first sight.

There were many differences between Mary Todd, who was raised in a wealthy family and had a formal education, and Lincoln, who was from a poor family and had to make it on his own.

However, the couple fell in love and were soon engaged.

Despite her father's persistent disapproval, Lincoln and Mary Todd were married at last in 1842.

From a Log Cabin to the White House

Track 01 ▶

After building his reputation as a lawyer for 10 years, Lincoln was elected to the House of Representatives and set out for Washington, D.C. to start his political career. That year, Abraham and Mary welcomed their second son. It was 3 years after their first son, Robert, was born. The young Lincoln family was very happy.

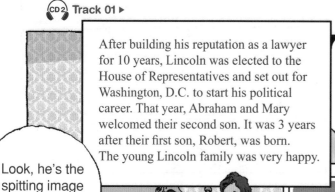

Look, he's the spitting image of you.

Mary, our son is so beautiful.

Ah! Let's name our son Edward Baker.

Edward Baker?

Yes. It's the name of a Congressman I respect and admire.

That's a good name, Edward Baker Lincoln!

He's wrinkly and ugly like a deflated balloon!

Their misfortune did not end there. Soon after, Lincoln's father, Thomas, passed away from an illness, and Lincoln fell into a severe depression.

Dear Husband, how long will you be like this?

You have so much to do. What about the work you dedicated your life to?

What's the use? It has nothing to do with me now.

Mr. Lincoln! Have you forgotten that little black girl in New Orleans? You, my husband, Abraham Lincoln, were the Very man, who with the saddest expression on his face, solemnly swore to find freedom for all black slaves!

I question how such a person like him became a Congressman.

Hmph! As a greenhorn with no political knowledge, how dare he!

How could I work side by side with such foolish and ignoble people!

Not even one person agreed with Lincoln's political convictions. As soon as his congressional term was over, the disappointed Lincoln returned to Springfield and vowed to devote himself solely to his legal career.

However, in 1854 an alarming event happened that changed Lincoln's determination not to dabble in politics again and fueled his re-entry to politics, stronger and more earnest than ever.

A controversial bill which allowed states to decide for themselves the issue of slavery was passed into law by Congress, repealing the Missouri Compromise, which had initially established that any territory joining the United States north of Missouri's border would be a free state and south of it would be a slave state.
This, in a sense, meant that all the states could essentially permit slavery.

Lincoln could not restrain his anger towards Stephen Douglas who had introduced, sponsored, and helped push such a bill into law. Thus, he reentered politics and ran for the U.S. Senate seat.

We must work to protect our Union. Freeing the slaves is a necessary act for this to occur!

Slavery is founded on the selfishness of man's nature!

We must not allow such an unjust and immoral institution to stand. We cannot forgive even those who merely tolerate and tacitly accept slavery.

Many people lent their ears to Lincoln's passionate speeches and applauded to show their approval, and yet, Lincoln lost his Senate race.

Don't be disappointed. You were great!

Thank you, Dear. Well, I'm satisfied enough knowing that people heard what I had to say.

However, Lincoln was not discouraged. He was glad that through his speeches, he had enlightened thousands of people on the injustice and cruelty of slavery.

"All men" as specified in the Declaration of Independence applies at best to white men only. Blacks are not men and cannot be equal to whites.

The Declaration of Independence firmly proclaims that all men are created equal. Accordingly, the claim that only whites are men goes against all reason!

Wherever Douglas went to make his pro-slavery argument, Lincoln followed to refute Douglas' views. This became known as the "Lincoln-Douglas Debates" and generated much discussions and opinions among the people. On the days the two debated, thousands of people gathered.

The number of supporters who were in line with Lincoln's political ideology was growing, and he soon became so famous nationally that everyone knew of his name.

But in his second try for the U.S. Senate, Lincoln lost to Douglas by an insignificant number of votes. This time he was dissapointed by the result.

I don't think I'm suited for politics.

You're giving up already? You can't. We are thinking of you as next year's presidential candidate.

I'm not suitable for such a position.

What nonsense! Don't you know how many countrymen are earnestly supporting you?

How can you say that after seeing today's election results? I'll drop out this time around.

You cannot quit, Congressman! You have to continue to fight.

How could you give up a such an important fight? Reclaiming fundamental human rights is our duty, is it not?

That's right! You must show them that justice will ultimately prevail.

Justice? Haven't you seen the society we live in? Don't you know that justice without power means nothing?

How could I have thought of abandoning such people? Even if I fail 100 times or even 1,000 times, I shall not give up, indeed!

In 1860, Lincoln was nominated as the Republican Party's presidential candidate, and he was again matched against Douglas.

One night, Lincoln received a letter from an 11-year-old girl.

Dear Mr. Lincoln!

I am Grace Bedell from Westfield, New York.
I want you to be President of the United States very much.
But your face as it appears on the poster is so thin and
not very handsome. If you will let your whiskers grow,
you would look a great deal better.
Then, everyone would vote for you.

She's right! I'm not too handsome, am I? Ha-ha-ha!

My Dear little Miss Grace,

Thank you!
You gave me some very important advice.
As you suggested, I'll try to grow whiskers.

That year, during the winter presidential election, Lincoln finally won over Douglas and became the 16th President of the United States of America.

Three cheers for President Lincoln!

Protector of freedom and peace!

Three cheers for Honest Abe!

Lincoln! Lincoln!

Even though Lincoln was born in a small log cabin on the frontier as a son of a poor settler and did not receive even one year of formal education, he was able to rise to the presidency with honesty and integrity, a strong will and convictions, and hard work.

After the inauguration on March 4, 1861, Lincoln made a triumphant entry into the White House as the President.

06 The Civil War

 Track 10 ▶

After Lincoln, who promised to abolish slavery, was elected the President, the Southern pro-slavery states, South Carolina, Mississippi, Florida, Alabama, Georgia, Louisiana, and Texas,...... seceded from the Union, declared their independence, and formed a new nation called the "Confederate States of America".

Jefferson Davis was elected their president. Afterwards, they declared war on the United States of America.

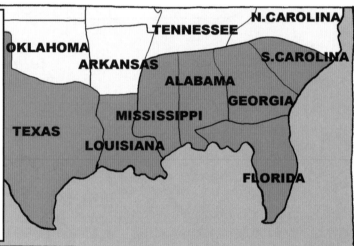

Sir, the Southern troops have besieged Fort Sumter in South Carolina. Currently, about 80 soldiers are isolated within the fort.

Convene the Cabinet members and General Winfield Scott immediately!

Yes, sir.

If we surrender, they will see us as weak. But if we confront them with an attack, other border states might also leave the Union.

What must be done?

However, as soon as the Northern relief fleet entered Charleston Harbor, Southern forces began their bombardment.

Just 40 days into Lincoln's presidency, the long dreaded war broke out. The Civil War, in which people of the same nation were aiming guns at one another, began.

It was beyond our capacity to defend ourselves against them. All the soldiers who survived scattered.

For certain, those were the only measures we could have taken...

The war was inevitable, Mr. President. Also, there are words that they may soon proceed northward.

Virginia just joined the Confederate States of America, and Richmond was chosen as their capital!

We have to strike first.

I understand. Call General George McClellan.

Yes, Sir.

Lincoln appointed McClellan as the Union's general-in-chief and ordered an attack on the Confederate capital, Richmond. Though McClellan was a skilled tactician and at times a brilliant strategist, he was an arrogant man.

Attack Richmond.

We don't have enough soldiers as it is. Please call up more troops.

If we recruit more soldiers, it will lead to the increase of people's anxiety and insecurities. If we just follow the plan…

With all due respect, do you think war is executed exactly as planned?

Even if you have never been to war, you should know better.

General, refrain from using disrespectful language towards the President!

The war continued on for more than a year, but Northern forces were being repeatedly defeated by Southern forces led by General Robert E. Lee.

How could such atrocious, bloody fighting continue within one nation?

Heavenly Father! I cannot abandon them. I will continue on until all the blacks become free men. Please help me to end this horrible war soon...

Lincoln often visited the hospitals of the wounded soldiers and comforted them.

There is nothing more we can do for him. Not only are his injuries too severe, but also he was transported here too late.

So you mean, you can't save him?

No, sir.

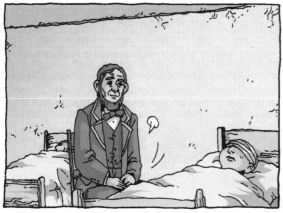

Is there anything I can do for you?

Therefore, though I may depart before I see you again, please do not be very sad.

I, Abraham Lincoln, write this letter on behalf of your beloved son.

Mr. President, a telegram is…

Shh!

President? Is this our President, Abraham Lincoln?

Yes, Son, and now that you know who I am, is there anything more I can do for you?

Nothing more, unless you can hold my hand and just let me hear your voice.

"Do not be terrified, do not be discouraged, for the Lord your God will be with you wherever you go."

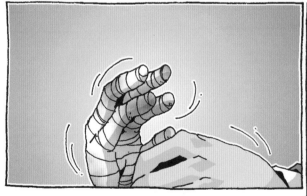

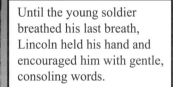

Until the young soldier breathed his last breath, Lincoln held his hand and encouraged him with gentle, consoling words.

The news and his son's death all came like a thunderbolt. Lincoln--who had already lost his second son--was now faced with the loss of his third son, William Wallace Lincoln.
His heart crumbled, and great sobs overcame him, shaking his body.

At the time when the outcomes of the battles were unfavorable for Northern forces, some surprising news came.

Mr. President! We-- We won!

What did you say?

It's done! At last, a victory!

General McClellan defeated the South!

Let's see.

128

Finally, in September of 1862, at the Battle of Antietam in Maryland, Northern troops won their first victory.

Immediately send a telegram to the General. Order him to pursue Southern troops at once. We must not give them any opportunity to escape.

Yes, sir!

Also, make sure to tell him that he did a fine job.

I'll do so.

John, I need to go to Antietam. Prepare to leave.

Lincoln, who finally heard the long-awaited victory news, went to the battlefield to praise the soldiers for their heroic efforts.

Thank you for serving our country!

It's my honor, Mr. President.

Thank you.

It's been an honor to serve you, Sir!

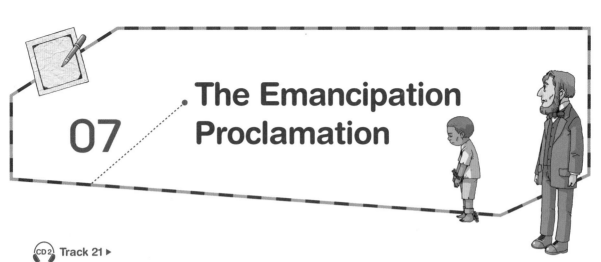

07 The Emancipation Proclamation

General McClellan, who had secured a victory, was eventually removed from his position. Lincoln appointed General George Meade as the new commander of the Union army. And Lincoln decided to settle once and for all a matter he had been laboring over for a long time, the issue of slave emancipation.

Today, I have reached a very important decision.

If slavery is not abolished, this country cannot stand.

If we continue to fight without abolishing slavery - the underlying cause of the war, this war will have been in vain.

I will free the black slaves!

No, in fact, all the slaves in the Union shall be freed!

That will invoke a greater insurrection in the South!

It's not the most favorable time to do so. Let's first monitor the affairs of the war and then decide.

How can you say that? With a victory in our hands, Now is the most opportune time.

Southern troops are increasingly growing in numbers. We need to break their morale.

This is like adding fuel to a burning house. Please reconsider.

My decision is final. I do not want your advice about the matter any longer. Meeting adjourned!

Having arrived at a decision, Lincoln wrote the proclamation after many edits and drafts.

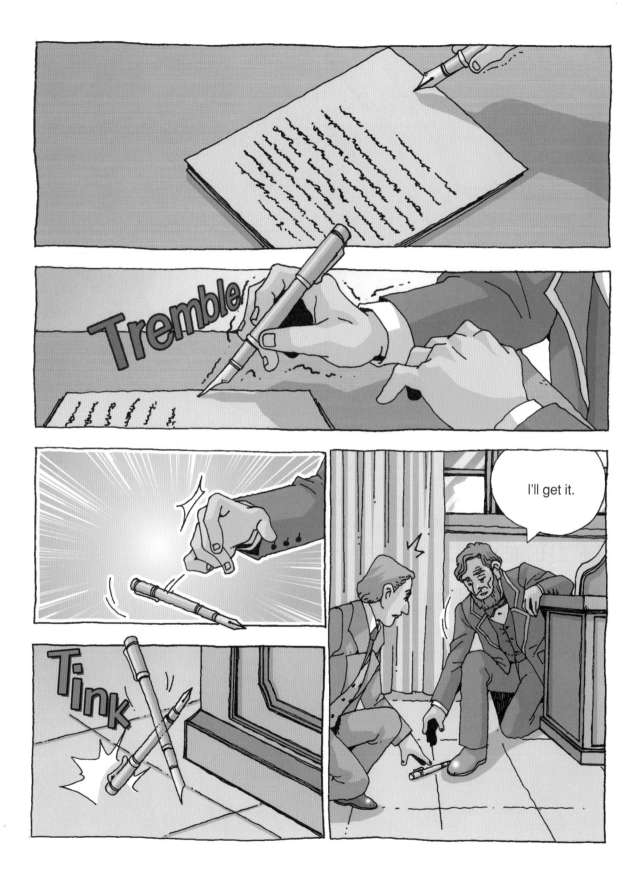

And my whole soul is in it. But if people noticed my hand trembling before signing the Proclamation,

won't all who examine this document hereafter say, "He hesitated"?

HA HA HA

That will do! Now, right or wrong, let's leave it to our country and to history.

On January 1, 1863, Lincoln issued the Emancipation Proclamation. This was one of the most momentous events that left a profound mark on American history. With this Proclamation, a new nation was born.

That on the 1st day of January, in 1863, all persons held as slaves within any State or designated part of a State, the people whereof shall then be in rebellion against the United States, shall be then, thenceforward, and forever free.

The Executive Government of the United States, including the military and naval authority, will recognize and maintain the freedom of such persons, and will do no act or acts to repress such persons, or any of them, in any efforts they may make for their actual freedom.

Now, I, Abraham Lincoln, President of the United States, on this 1st day of January, in 1863, do publicly proclaimed for 100 days, from the day first above mentioned, order and designate as the States and parts of States that are this day in rebellion against the United States, the following: Arkansas, Texas, Louisiana, Mississippi, Alabama, Florida, Georgia, South Carolina, North Carolina, and Virginia.

I do order and declare that all persons held as slaves within said designated States, and parts of States, are, and henceforward shall be free; and that the Executive government of the United States, including the military and naval authorities, will recognize and maintain the freedom of said persons.

And I hereby enjoin upon the people so declared to be free to abstain from all violence, unless in necessary self-defense; and I recommend to them that they labor faithfully for reasonable wages.

And I further declare and make known, that they will be received into the armed service of the United States to garrison forts, positions, stations, and other places, and to man vessels of all sorts.

Issuing of the Proclamation brought much jubilation among supporters of the abolition of slavery and the black slaves who were now freed from their chains and shackles.
But, the resistance by the South increased significantly.

So if we meet the requirements, we can enlist in the army?

You're saying that we can be United States soldiers, too?

Hey, then let's go and join the Union army right away.

Definitely! Since the President has freed us, we need to lend our support in return.

In the midst of all the violent fighting, the number of casualties continued to climb. The morale of the Union troops hit rock bottom as the South continued to defeat them.

General, we must retreat. Please order the retreat!

Reinforcements will be arriving soon. Sir, we need to hold out until then.

Retreat! Tell the entire army to retreat!

141

With no signs of the war ending, Lincoln became anxious and restless.

General Lee of the South is leading a large army of 75,000 men into Pennsylvania.

Are the Union troops still in Maryland?

Yes, sir.

The outcome of this war will be decided by this battle.

We must stop them at all costs!

Yes, sir!

On July 1, 1863, the Civil War's bloodiest battle erupted in a small town of Gettysburg.

The countless corpses of the dead soldiers were mounting, and the ground of Gettysburg was drenched in blood.

144

We need to make a cemetery to honor them.

Yes, sir.

Lincoln headed to Gettysburg to create a cemetery for the fallen soldiers and to dedicate a memorial service for them.

On November 19, 1863, more than 15,000 mourners gathered at Gettysburg.

We are met on a great battlefield of that war.

We have come to dedicate a portion of that field, as a final resting place for those who here gave their lives that that nation might live.

From these honored dead we take increased devotion to that cause for which they gave the last full measure of devotion,

that we here highly resolve that these dead shall not have died in vain.

Although Lincoln's address was very short, lasting a little over 2 minutes, it left an indelible and profound impression on everyone.

General Meade, who had led the Union army to victory at Gettysburg, was reluctant to pursue General Lee on a pretext that his troops were too tired and exhausted. In the meantime, the cornered Southern troops were able to retreat.

It's too difficult. Please allow us to rest.

It's a golden opportunity to put an end to this war.

But isn't the morale of the troops higher than ever?

Due to the Gettysburg battle, the soldiers are very exhausted. And the wounded soldiers need to be treated.

I see.

Lincoln retired General Meade and appointed General Ulysses Grant as the new general-in-chief of all the armies of the United States. He was an upright general whose drive and tenacity were unmatched.

Nevertheless, the war continued on, and there were no indications of an end to the war.

The Legacy of Freedom and Equality

08

Because of the casualties from the unending war, many people were in despair over the continuous enlistment.
They began to voice their doubts over Lincoln's leadership.

Aren't they ever exhausted? They are advancing north unceasingly.

I want to go home.

Who wouldn't? Who is this war for anyways?

In September 1864, 3 years after the war began, the news of the North's victory came streaming in. With a win in Atlanta, Georgia, the key turning point in the war, Northern troops began to conquer the Southern states one by one.

With those victories, people's doubts over Lincoln's leadership faded, and Lincoln was reelected as the 17th President of the United States.

YEAH!

Hurray!

On April 3, 1864, one month after Lincoln was inaugurated as President, Northern troops captured Richmond, the capital city of Confederate States of America.

I need to go to Richmond.

At last, the Confederate General-in-Chief Lee surrendered. The devastating Civil War, which lasted for 4 years taking 600,000 lives, was finally over. Pursuant to Lincoln's Emancipation Proclamation, the Southern black slaves were all freed.

The war is over!

It's finally over!

Hooray!

Hooray!

YAHOO

CD 2 Track 34 ▸

Look at this city desolated by the war.
The war left a big wound in all of us.
This is not the time to decide over right or wrong but to combine our forces to reconstruct our destroyed city.
Then are you going to pardon the Southerners?
I have already pardoned them.
because they are our brothers.

159

On April 14, 1865, Lincoln went to the Ford's Theater to see a play with his wife.

CLAP CLAP CLAP

Henry, sit down. Enjoy the play!

Yes, Mr. President!

Clara, I hope you and your fiancé will like the play.

Thank you for inviting us.

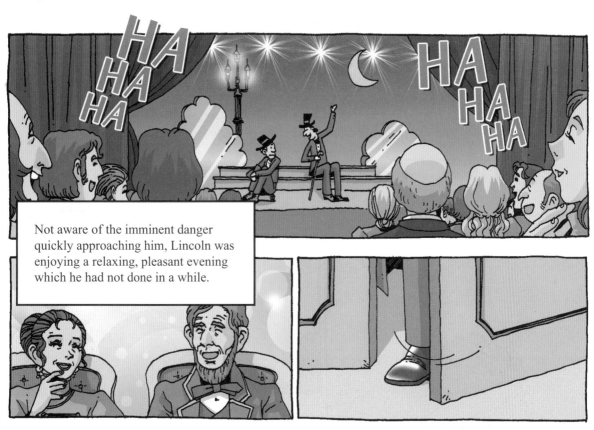

Not aware of the imminent danger quickly approaching him, Lincoln was enjoying a relaxing, pleasant evening which he had not done in a while.

At a time when the play was in full swing in the midst of a comical scene, a gunshot rang out over the audience's laughter inside the Ford's Theater.

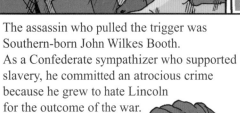

The assassin who pulled the trigger was Southern-born John Wilkes Booth.
As a Confederate sympathizer who supported slavery, he committed an atrocious crime because he grew to hate Lincoln for the outcome of the war.

The president's been shot!

Call the doctor!

The fatally wounded Lincoln was moved to a house across the street from the Ford's Theater.

Lincoln was buried in Springfield, Illinois where his political career first began.
Because millions of mourners came to Lincoln's funeral procession to pay their last respects, it took several weeks just to transport his body to Springfield.

Lincoln was born to a poor settler. He studied on his own through books and worked hard in life. In his twenties, he took on his business partner's huge debt, which most people would have forsaken without hesitation. Instead, he worked faithfully and diligently to repay it and earned many people's trust. After Lincoln entered politics, he suffered several setbacks and failed. And yet, he pushed forward and fought until he surpassed his obstacles.

Believing that "all men are free and equal," Lincoln freed the black slaves. Also after winning the Civil War, he showed compassion and magnanimity to all and even embraced his enemies. Although he himself experienced heart-wrenching pain, he consoled others and considered their needs and pain first. Never losing hope for the nation's future despite personally struggling with endless sorrows, Abraham Lincoln was and is still highly respected as one of the greatest presidents in the history of America.

Word Search

● Find the words which are hidden horizontally, vertically and diagonally.

```
Q M Z G Q M Z G Q M Z G Q Q M Z G Q M Z
W S E C E S S I O N A H W W N A H W N L
E B Q J E B Q J E B Q J E E B Q J E B E
P V C K R V C K R V C K R R V P K R V G
R C D L T C D L T C D L T T C R L T C I
E X E Q Y X E Q Y X E Q Y Y X E Q Y X S
C Z V W U D V W U Z V W U U Z S W U Z L
E A R E I A E E I A R E I I A E E I A A
D S G R O S G F O S G R O O S R R O S T
E D H T P D H T E D H T P P D V T P D O
N F U Y A F U Y A A U Y A A F E Y A F R
T G I U S G I U S G T U S S G I U S G I
D H O I D H O I D H O I D D H O I D H O
F J T J F J T J F J T J F F J T E F J T
G K A M O M E N T O U S A U E N H L E
H L B N H L E N H L E N H H U E N H L E
J Q O M J Q T M J Q T M J T Q T M J Q T
L W L Q L W Y Q S T R I V E W Y Q L W Y
Z W I F Z W K F Z W K S Z Z W K F Z W K
X E S U X E M U X E M U X X E M U X E M
C R H C C R Q C C R Q C C C R Q C C R Q
```

legislator	secession	defeat	precedent
momentous	strive	abolish	preserve

Vocabulary

● Match each word to the correct meaning.

1. defend   • 동맹

2. conviction   • 겸손한

3. union   • 연설

4. opponent   • 신념

5. equality   • 방어하다

6. perish   • 반대하는

7. White House   • 자유

8. emancipation   • 평등

9. proclamation   • 사라지다

10. liberty   • 노예 해방

11. address   • 선언

12. humble   • 백악관

Guess What?

• Guess what he said in the blank.

U.S. Presidents Quiz

1. Who was the first president to ride in an automobile?

1) Andrew Jackson   2) Theodore Roosevelt   3) Thomas Jefferson

Theodore Roosevelt(1901-1909) was the first President to ride in a car.

2. Which President was the first president to ride in an airplane?

1) Franklin Roosevelt   2) Warren Harding   3) Herbert Hoover

Franklin Roosevelt(1933-1945) was the first President to ride in an airplane.

3. Which President wrote the Declaration of Independence?

1) John Adams   2) William Harrison   3) Thomas Jefferson

Thomas Jefferson (1801-1809) wrote most of the Declaration of independence. He was George Washington's Secretary of State.

4. Which president said, "Ask not what your country can do for you, but what you can do for your country?" ?

1) Richard M. Nixon   2) Bill Clinton   3) John F. Kennedy

John F. Kennedy(1961-1963) spoke these famous words in his 1961 inaugural address.

5. Who issued the Emancipation Proclamation?

1) Abraham Lincoln   2) Benjamin Harrison   3) George Washington

The Emancipation Proclamation for freeing the slaves was issued in 1862, and Abraham Lincoln (1860-65) was the President at that time.

6. Which president had been a Hollywood actor?

1) Bill Cliton   2) Ronald Reagon   3) George Bush

Ronald Reagan (1981-1989) starred in more than 50 movies.

List of Presidents

1st

George Washington
(1789-1797)

3rd

Thomas Jefferson
(1801-1809)

7th

Andrew Jackson
(1829-1837)

11th

James Knox Polk
(1795-1849)

16th

Abraham Lincoln
(1861-1865)

26th

Theodore Roosevelt
(1901-1909)

32nd

Franklin D. Roosevelt
(1933-1945)

40th

Ronald Reagan
(1981-1989)

41st

George H. W. Bush
(1989-1993)

The United States of America had a variety of different Presidents throughout its history. The Presidents are from different places, with different ideals, with different personalities, in different times. But they all do grand roles to make the history of America. Belows are the list of U.S. Presidents in chronological order.

Bill Clinton
(1993-2001)

George W. Bush
(2001-2009)

Barack Obama
(2009-   )

1st	George Washington (1789-1797)		23rd	Benjamin Harrison (1889-1893)
2nd	John Adams (1797-1801)		24th	Grover Cleveland (1893-1897)
3rd	Thomas Jefferson (1801-1809)		25th	William McKinley (1897-1901)
4th	James Madison (1809-1817)		26th	Theodore Roosevelt (1901-1909)
5th	James Monroe (1817-1825)		27th	William H. Taft (1909-1913)
6th	John Quincy Adams (1825-1829)		28th	Woodrow Wilson (1913-1921)
7th	Andrew Jackson (1829-1837)		29th	Warren G. Harding (1921-1923)
8th	Martin Van Buren (1837-1841)		30th	Calvin Coolidge (1923-1929)
9th	William H.Harrison (1841-1841)		31st	Herbert Hoover (1929-1933)
10th	John Tyler (1841-1845)		32nd	Franklin D. Roosevelt (1933-1945)
11th	James K. Polk (1845-1849)		33rd	Harry S. Truman (1945-1953)
12th	Zachary Taylor (1849-1850)		34th	Dwight D. Eisenhower (1953-1961)
13th	Millard Fillmore (1850-1853)		35th	John F. Kennedy (1961-1963)
14th	Franklin Pierce (1853-1857)		36th	Lyndon B. Johnson (1963-1969)
15th	James Buchanan (1857-1861)		37th	Richard M. Nixon (1969-1974)
16th	Abraham Lincoln (1861-1865)		38th	Garald Ford (1974-1977)
17th	Andrew Johnson (1865-1869)		39th	Jimmy Carter (1977-1981)
18th	Ulysses S. Grant (1869-1877)		40th	Ronald Reagan (1981-1989)
19th	Rutherford B. Hayes (1877-1881)		41st	George H. W. Bush (1989-1993)
20th	James A Garfield (1881-1881)		42nd	Bill Clinton (1993-2001)
21st	Chester A. Arthur (1881-1885)		43rd	George W. Bush (2001-2009)
22nd	Grover Cleveland (1885-1889)		44th	Barack Obama (2009-)

1809년   2월 12일, 미국 켄터키 주에서 태어났습니다.

1815년 6세   인근의 작은 학교에 다니며 책을 접하게 됩니다.

1818년 9세   어머니 낸시 링컨이 병으로 세상을 떠납니다.

1819년 10세   아버지의 재혼으로 새어머니 사라 부시 존스턴과 가족이 됩니다.

1827년 18세   오하이오 강에서 뱃사공 일을 합니다.

1831년 22세   덴튼의 부탁으로 뉴올리언스까지 동행합니다.
                       그곳에서 노예 시장을 보고 노예 해방이라는 평생의 목표를 세웁니다.

1832년 23세   일리노이 주 주의원 선거에 휘그당원으로 출마하지만 낙선합니다.
                       윌리엄 베리와 동업으로 상점을 엽니다.

1833년 24세   상점이 문을 닫고 동업자가 사망하자 많은 빚을 떠안게 됩니다.
                       뉴 세일럼의 우체국장이 됩니다.

1834년 25세   휘그당원으로 일리노이 주 주의원에 당선됩니다.

1837년 28세   독학으로 법률 공부를 하여 변호사 시험에 통과합니다.
                       제 2의 고향인 스프링필드로 이사를 합니다.

1840년 31세   정부통령 선거 위원에 출마하지만 낙선합니다.

1842년 33세	메리 토드와 결혼을 합니다.
1846년 37세	하원 의원에 당선되어 워싱턴으로 진출합니다.
1847년 38세	노예 해방을 주장하지만 의원들의 냉대로 좌절합니다. 하원 의원직을 마치고 변호사 일에만 매진합니다.
1854년 45세	공화당에 입당해 상원 의원 선거에 출마하지만 민주당의 스티븐 더글러스에게 패합니다.
1858년 49세	다시 상원 의원 선거에 입후보하지만 낙선합니다.
1860년 51세	미국 16대 대통령에 당선됩니다.
1861년 52세	노예 제도를 찬성하는 남부 7개 주가 미국 연방 탈퇴를 선언하고 남부 연합국을 세웁니다. 남부군의 포트 섬터 공격으로 남북 전쟁이 시작됩니다.
1862년 53세	메릴랜드 주의 안티텀 전투에서 북부군이 처음으로 승리합니다.
1863년 54세	노예 해방 선언문을 발표합니다.
1864년 55세	미국 17대 대통령으로 재선됩니다.
1865년 56세	4월 9일, 남부군의 항복으로 남북 전쟁이 끝납니다. 4월 14일, 워싱턴의 포드 극장에서 연극을 보던 중, 존 윌크스 부스의 총에 맞습니다. 4월 15일, 숨을 거둡니다.

who? 01	Barack Obama	979-11-5639-023-7
who? 02	Charles Darwin	979-11-5639-024-4
who? 03	Bill Gates	979-11-5639-025-1
who? 04	Hillary Clinton	979-11-5639-026-8
who? 05	Stephen Hawking	979-11-5639-027-5
who? 06	Oprah Winfrey	979-11-5639-028-2
who? 07	Steven Spielberg	979-11-5639-029-9
who? 08	Thomas Edison	979-11-5639-030-5
who? 09	Abraham Lincoln	979-11-5639-031-2
who? 10	Martin Luther King, Jr.	979-11-5639-032-9
who? 11	Louis Braille	979-11-5639-033-6
who? 12	Albert Einstein	979-11-5639-034-3
who? 13	Jane Goodall	979-11-5639-035-0
who? 14	Walt Disney	979-11-5639-036-7
who? 15	Winston Churchill	979-11-5639-037-4
who? 16	Warren Buffett	979-11-5639-008-4
who? 17	Nelson Mandela	979-11-5639-009-1
who? 18	Steve Jobs	979-11-5639-010-7
who? 19	J. K. Rowling	979-11-5639-011-4
who? 20	Jean-Henri Fabre	979-11-5639-012-1
who? 21	Vincent van Gogh	979-11-5639-013-8
who? 22	Marie Curie	979-11-5639-014-5
who? 23	Henry David Thoreau	979-11-5639-015-2
who? 24	Andrew Carnegie	979-11-5639-016-9
who? 25	Coco Chanel	979-11-5639-017-6
who? 26	Charlie Chaplin	979-11-5639-018-3
who? 27	Ho Chi Minh	979-11-5639-019-0
who? 28	Ludwig van Beethoven	979-11-5639-020-6
who? 29	Mao Zedong	979-11-5639-021-3
who? 30	Kim Dae-jung	979-11-5639-022-0

Biography Comic who?